THE UNDYING SPIRIT OF FRANCE

THE UNDYING SPIRIT OF FRANCE

LES TRAITS ÉTERNELS DE LA FRANCE

BY MAURICE BARRÈS

TRANSLATED BY
MARGARET W. B. CORWIN
WITH A FOREWORD BY
THEODORE STANTON

NEW HAVEN
YALE UNIVERSITY PRESS
LONDON: HUMPHREY MILFORD
OXFORD UNIVERSITY PRESS
MDCCCCXVII

COPYRIGHT, 1917, BY
YALE UNIVERSITY PRESS

First published, October, 1917.
Second printing, February, 1918.
Third printing, May, 1918.

FOREWORD

M. Maurice Barrès is a man of such varied interest that he might well be studied from more than one point of view. I shall concentrate my attention, however, particularly to that side of his character shown in his activities as a writer, with a brief glance at those as politician and patriot.

As a writer M. Barrès stands unquestionably in the front rank of living French authors. His ability for marshalling facts is unexcelled, while his style of expression has seldom been equalled. At times his ideas may not coincide with ours, but we can never fail to recognize the skill and charm with which they are presented. The following pages seem to me to reflect, even in translation, his choice diction and the masterly arrangement of his material. Indeed his gifts of style have been considered remarkable by the best critics of

France. M. Paul Desjardins spoke of him in the late twenties as "that youth endowed with remarkable diction," M. Charles Maurras writes of "the music of Barrès's prose," while M. Henri Bremond, in what is to me the finest critical study of Barrès written up to ten years ago, the preface to "Vingt-cinq Années de Vie Littéraire," devotes a section to "Barrès's rhythm." M. Anatole France, reviewing one of M. Barrès's books, says: "His language is supple and at the same time precise; it has wonderful resources."

It is interesting to note what Barrès himself says on the same subject. "The art of writing must satisfy these two requirements—it must be musical and meet the demand for mathematical precision, which exists among the French in every well-regulated soul."

As a British journalist and author, the Hon. Maurice Baring, points out, M. Barrès's "early books are written in an elaborate style and are often obscure." As he advanced in life and experience, however, his style became less involved and the obscurity disappeared completely, as the readers of the following pages can confirm. In this respect he reverses the course of one of his admirers, Henry James, who began his literary career with a clear style and clear thought and ended with both bathed in ambiguity.

Hero-worship also stands out prominently in M. Maurice Barrès's writings. To him all "exceptional men" are heroes. He is very catholic in his choice of them, numbering in his earlier books those as varied as Napoleon, Renan and Taine. Later Boulanger and Déroulède became his chief worthies. With the coming of the war M. Barrès attains the climax of his reverence for exceptional men, for it is at the shrine of the martyr soldier boys of France that he worships, as we shall see in the pages that follow. Here, as in the matter of style, his taste mellows with age.

Considering Barrès as a patriot and politician, we are almost tempted to pronounce him the Roosevelt of France. There are indeed marks of resemblance between these two "exceptional men," in their character, ideas, books and activities. For Barrès, like Roosevelt, is an ardent disciple of the doctrine of "the strenuous life." Thus, in the preface to "L'Ennemi des Lois," we read: "It is not systems which we lack, but energy,—the energy to conform our habits to our way of thinking." His "Déracinés" has been called by him "a novel of national energy."

Barrès's excessive patriotism is also Rooseveltian in many respects. He was born in Lorraine in 1862 and was consequently but a child when the Provinces were torn from France in 1871. His native region is ever in his mind and heart, and stands out conspicuously in all his writings. In the preface to "Au Service de l'Allemagne," he says: "The author being a French Lorrainer necessarily judges everything from the standpoint of Lorraine and France." Note how he puts Lorraine even before

France. It appears in his very first book. In his latest volume, "Les Diverses Familles Spirituelles de la France," Lorraine is not forgotten. In his most recent essay, that in the July *Atlantic Monthly,* it is continually appearing, nor is it absent from the oration which follows.

I recall the presence of Barrès at Rennes during the famous Dreyfus trial of 1899. He represented a Paris daily to which he sent, nightly, long telegrams, and I performed a like duty for an American cable syndicate. But we were in opposite camps and did not speak. I still see his sparse figure of medium height and not yet touched with the *embonpoint* of the forties, leaning over the back of the bench in front of him, his swarthy face crowned with heavy dark hair which shaded his deep-set piercing eyes, following attentively every word, and intonation, and phrase of those heart-moving depositions.

Of late M. Barrès has frequently expressed the hope that the *"union sacrée,*" created by the present war, would continue after the peace. "Is it possible," he asks, "that the same forces which, only yesterday, precipitated us, one against the other, but which the mobilization checked,—is it possible that this is all to begin again? Yes, but this time not for the purpose of dividing us or with any aim of exclusion; this time will be founded on our diversity the finest and most active amity. . . . The only diversities which now exist are those which spring from our nature and history. . . . To-day France is unified and purified."

Our entrance into the war has been balm in Gilead to the patriotic soul of Barrès and has deepened his old warmth of feeling for America. As I am correcting the proofs of this preface, he sends me this message from his native Charmes, in the Vosges: "In this corner of Lorraine where I am writing you, and where during the night we hear the rumble of our victorious cannon, I am the neighbor of your first contingent.

Give us five hundred thousand as good as these ten or twenty thousand superb soldiers, and our common foe will begin to make a wry face."

During the past year or two, M. Barrès has made the home letters of the young French heroes at the front his special contribution to the literature of the war. Besides the splendid ones given in the pages which follow, similar ones may be found in the *Atlantic* article already referred to, and in "Les Diverses Familles Spirituelles de la France," where they form the woof and warp of the text, while others are scattered through the pages of the half dozen volumes made up of his remarkable articles contributed to the Paris daily, *L'Echo de Paris,* and brought together under the collective title, "L'Ame Française et la Guerre." Still others appear in some of the many prefaces which M. Barrès has added to the war books of his friends.

Some surprise may be occasioned in the minds of those of a skeptical turn of thought at the apparently inexhaustible stock of these letters. Whence does M. Barrès get all these epistles *d'outre tombe?* In "Les Diverses Familles Spirituelles de la France," M. Barrès himself answers this question when he speaks of "the millions of sublime letters, which, for the past two years, have furnished France her spiritual food, . . . these innumerable letters, perhaps a million a day." And it should be remembered that the number of young men at the front who write them is an almost constant number and will continue to be so until the end of the war, for each year the new "class," composed mostly of boys from nineteen to twenty, enters upon its military duties in the trenches.

Other readers of these letters may ask whether all the soldier boys of France write like those presented to the public by M. Barrès. Without giving a direct answer to this question, I may say that everybody who is in close touch with the noble France of to-day has had experiences similar to those of M. Barrès.

During the first fourteen months of this war I served as an orderly in a large military hospital near Paris where we had some six hundred wounded. My duties were to write letters for those young Frenchmen who were incapacitated in any way from writing for themselves, and I can say that I often helped to put on paper just such thoughts as those found in the letters revealed to us by M. Barrès, while during my present sojourn in the United States I have received directly or indirectly letters of this same tenor.

Thus, a retired artillery officer, Major Levylier, of Décauville, Calvados, wrote me last winter:

"My son, Lieutenant Paul Levylier, of the 25th regiment of dragoons, was completing his second year in architecture at the Paris School of Fine Arts, when the war broke out. At the moment of mobilization he wrote to his elder sister and asked her in case of his death to request me to give the necessary capital to found a prize at the school; which I have done. His letter ended with these words for the rest of the family: 'Tell them to close their eyes; then you kiss them and they will think it is I.' He died bravely in Champagne on October 6, 1915, crushed by a shell, at the head of his platoon. His last words to his captain were: 'Tell Father that I died for France.'"

M. Charles Torquet, the Paris dramatist and the literary executor of the young poet, Jacques de Choudens, severely wounded in August, 1914, and killed the following June, sends me these words which this superb youth wrote from the front to his grandmother: "If I do not come back, find consolation in this grander thought that I have contributed in my humble way to make thee more proud to be a French woman."

Another youthful soldier-poet, Gustave Rouger, sends me from a military hospital in the south of France, where he is convalescing, these lines, which seem to breathe a premonition like that also expressed by Jacques de Choudens when he was on the point of returning to the front, that he "may never come back," and which end a long poem, still in manuscript, which has just been awarded the literary prize of the Paris Society of Men of Letters:

> Quand éclatera la fleur épanouie,
> Avant que d'Ici-bas ma pauvre âme s'enfuie,
> Ah, laissez-moi chanter, mon Dieu, chanter toujours,
> Avec tout mon élan vers la sainte demeure,
> Où vos bras s'ouvriront pour m'accueillir un jour,
> Ah, laissez-moi chanter, avant que je ne meure,
> L'Eternelle Beauté dans l'Eternel Amour.

THEODORE STANTON.

Cornell Campus, October, 1917.

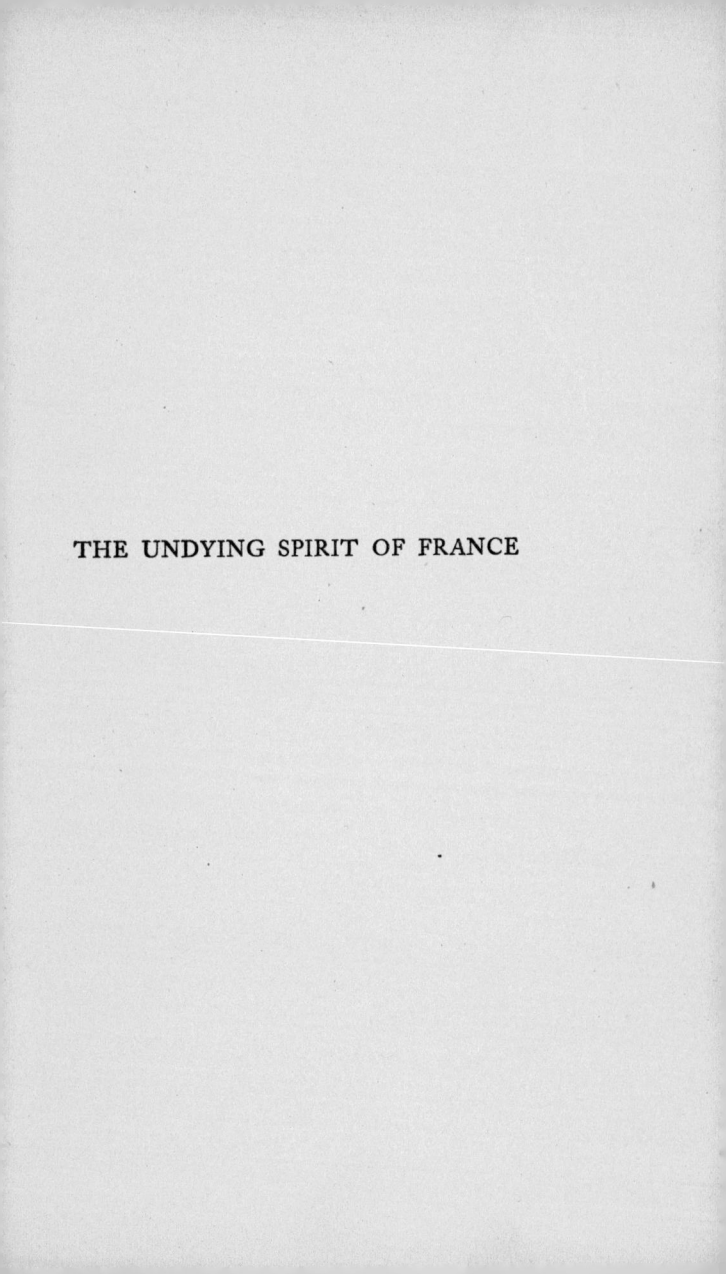

THE UNDYING SPIRIT OF FRANCE

THE UNDYING SPIRIT OF FRANCE

An Address delivered in London, at the Hall of the Royal Society, under the auspices of the British Academy, July 12, 1916.

Ladies and Gentlemen:

In his Litany of Nations your poet Swinburne puts these words into the mouth of France apostrophizing Liberty:

I am she that was thy sign and standard-bearer,
    Thy voice and cry;
She that washed thee with her blood and left thee fairer,
    The same was I.
Were not these the hands that raised thee fallen and fed thee,
    These hands defiled?
Was not I thy tongue that spake, thine eye that led thee,
    Not I thy child?

How many men and how many nations, since 1870, have believed that we were unworthy of this eulogy that so touched our hearts. We were mistrusted. They said of us: "They are no longer what they were . . . France is a nation grown old, an ancient nation."

Especial stress was laid upon the idea of France as an *old nation*. And therein they expressed but the truth; France was when no such thing existed as Germanic consciousness, or Italian or English consciousness; in truth we were the first nation of all Europe to grasp the idea of constituting a home-land; but there seems no reason why claims of such a nature should work to our discredit with nations of more recent origin.

Among those who thus spoke there were many who looked upon us without animosity, sometimes even with sympathy. According to them France had in the past laid up a vast store of virtues, noble deeds, and glorious achievements beyond compare, but to-day is seated in the midst of these like an old man in the evening of the most successful of lives, or still more like certain worldly aristocrats of illustrious lineage, who have preserved of their inheritance only their titles of nobility, charming manners, superb portraits, regal tapestries and books adorned with coats of arms, all denoting sumptuous but trivial luxury.

It was in this wise, as we well understand, that we had come to be regarded as jaded triflers, far too affluent and light-hearted, with pleasure as our only concern; the French people were supposed to allow impulse and passion to determine the course of their lives, pleasure being the supreme good sought, and to Paris came representatives from every nation to share in this pleasure.

Small wonder that the undiscerning foreigner, intoxicated by the easy and cosmopolitan pleasures of Paris, failed to recognize the underlying force present at every French fireside, which prides itself upon keeping remote and isolated from the passing crowd, or what was stirring in hearts ever hearkening the call to a crusade and needing, as it were, but the voice from a supernatural world to bring forth and reveal to themselves their inherent heroism.

I

August, 1914. The call to arms resounds. The bells in every village echo in the towers of the ancient churches whose foundations arise from amidst the dead. These bells have suddenly become the voice of the land of France. They call together the men, they express compassion for the women; their clamor is so stupendous that it seems as if the very tombs would crumble, and all at once the French heart is unlocked and all the tenderness that has so long been kept concealed comes forth.

Women, old men and children flock about the soldier, following him to the train. This is the hour of departure, not as Rude has depicted it,—carried along in the storm and stress of the *Marseillaise,* but a departure even more tragic in tone, in which the soldier mutters through set teeth: "Since they will have it, we must end it forever."

The departure! We cannot be at the same moment in all the railroad stations of Paris and of all our cities, towns and villages, on all the docks, nor upon all the boats bringing back loyal Frenchmen from abroad. Suppose we go to the very heart of military France, to the school of Saint Cyr where the young officers receive their training.

Every year at Saint Cyr the *Fête du Triomphe* is celebrated with great pomp. Upon this occasion is performed a traditional ceremony in which the young men who have just finished their two years' course at the school proceed to christen the class following it and bestow a name upon their juniors.

In July, 1914, this ceremony came just at the time of the events which in their hasty course brought on the war, and for that reason was to assume a more than usually serious character.

On the thirty-first of the month the general in command at the school made known to the *Montmirails* (the name of the graduating class), that they would have to christen their juniors that same evening, and only according to military regulations, without the accustomed festivities.

All understood that perhaps during the night they would have to join their respective regiments.

Listen to the words of a young poet of the *Montmirail* class, Jean Allard-Méeus, as he tells his mother of the events of this evening, already become legendary among his compatriots: "After dinner the Assumption of Arms (*prise d'armes*) before the captain and the lieutenant on guard duty, the only officers entitled to witness this sacred rite. A lovely evening; the air is filled with almost oppressive fragrance; the most perfect order prevails amidst unbroken silence. The *Montmirails* are drawn up, officers with swords, 'men' with guns. The two classes take their places on the parade ground under command of the major of the higher class. Excellent patriotic addresses, then, in the midst of growing emotion, I recited

'To-morrow'

Soldiers of our illustrious race,
   Sleep, for your memories are sublime.
Old time erases not the trace
   Of famous names graved on the tomb.
Sleep; beyond the frontier line
   Ye soon will sleep, once more at home.

"Never again, dearest mother, shall I repeat those lines, for never again shall I be on the eve of departure for out there, amongst a thousand young men trembling with feverish excitement, pride and hatred. Through my own emotion I must have touched upon a responsive chord, for I ended my verses amidst a general thrill. Oh, why did not the clarion sound the Call to Arms at their close! We should all have carried its echoes with us as far as the Rhine."

It was surrounded by this atmosphere of enthusiasm that the young officers received the title of *Croix du Drapeau* for their class upon their promotion and it was at this juncture that one of the *Montmirails,* Gaston Voizard, cried out: "Let us swear to go into battle in full dress uniform, with white gloves and the plume (*casoar*) in our hats."

"We swear it," made answer the five hundred of the *Montmirail.*

"We swear it," echoed the voices of the five hundred of the *Croix du Drapeau.*

A terrible scene and far too characteristically French, permeated by the admirable innocence and readiness to serve of these young men, and permeated, likewise, with disastrous consequences.

They kept their rash vow. It is not permissible for me to tell you the proportion of those who thus met death. These attractive boys of whom I have been telling you are no more. How have they fallen?

There were not witnesses in all cases, but they all met death in the same way as did Lieutenant de Fayolle.

On the twenty-second of August Alain de Fayolle of the *Croix du Drapeau* was at Charleroi leading a section. His men hesitate. The young sub-lieutenant has put on his white gloves but discovers that he has forgotten his plume. He draws from his saddle-bag the red and white plume and fastens it to his shako.

"You will get killed, my lieutenant," protested a corporal.

"Forward!" shouts the young officer.

His men follow him, electrified. A few moments later a bullet strikes him in the middle of his forehead, just below the plume.

On the same day, August 22, 1914, fell Jean Allard-Méeus, the poet of the *Montmirail,* struck by two bullets.

Gaston Voizard, the youth who suggested the vow, outlived them by only a few months. He seems to offer apologies for this in the charming and heart-breaking letter which follows.

December 25, 1914.
"It is midnight, Mademoiselle and good friend, and in order to write to you I have just removed my white gloves. (This is not a bid for admiration. The act has nothing of the heroic about it; my last colored pair adorn the hands of a poor foot-soldier (*piou-piou*) who was cold.)

"I am unable to find words to express the pleasure and emotion caused me by your letter which arrived on the evening following a terrific bombardment of the poor little village which we are holding. The letter was accepted among us as balm for all possible racking of nerves and other curses. That letter, which was read in the evening to the officers of my battalion,—I ask pardon for any offence to your modesty, —comforted the most cast down after the hard day and gave proof to all that the heart of the young girls of France is nothing short of magnificent in its beneficence.

"It is, as I have said, midnight. To the honor and good fortune which have come to me of commanding my company during the last week, (our captain having been wounded), I owe the pleasure of writing you at this hour from the trenches, where, by prodigies of cunning, I have succeeded in lighting a candle without attracting the attention of the gentlemen facing us, who are, by the way, not more than a hundred meters distant.

"My men, under their breath, have struck up the traditional Christmas hymn, 'He is born, the Child Divine.' The sky glitters with stars. One feels like making merry over all this, and, behold, one is on the brink of tears. I think of Christmases of other years spent with my family; I think of the tremendous effort still to be made, of the small chance I have for coming out of this alive; I think, in short, that perhaps this minute I am living my last Christmas.

"Regret, do you say? . . . No, not even sadness. Only a tinge of gloom at not being among all those I love.

"All the sorrow of my thoughts is given to those best of friends fallen on the field of honor, whose loyal affection had made them almost my brothers;— Allard, Fayolle, so many dear friends whom I shall never see again! When on the evening of July 31, in my capacity of *Père Système* of the Class of 1914 (promotion), I had pronounced amidst a holy hush the famous vow to make ourselves conspicuous by facing death wearing white gloves, our goodhearted Fayolle, who was, I may say, the most of an enthusiast of all the friends I have ever known, said to me with a grin: 'What a stunning impression we shall make upon the *Boches!* They will be so astounded that they will forget to fire.' But, alas, poor Fayolle has paid dearly his debt to his country for the title of Saint-Cyrien! And they are all falling around me, seeming to ask when the turn of their *Père Système* is to come, so that *Montmirail* on entering Heaven may receive God's blessing with full ranks.

"But a truce to useless repinings! Let us give thought only to our dear France, our indispensable, imperishable, everliving country! And, by this beauteous Christmas night, let us put our faith more firmly than ever in victory.

"I must ask you, Mademoiselle and good friend, to excuse this awful scrawl. Will you also allow me to hope for a reply in the near future and will you permit this young French officer very respectfully to kiss the hand of a great souled and generous-hearted maiden of France?"

On the eighth of April, 1915, came his turn to fall.

Ah, how dearly has France ever paid for the flaunting of these bits of bravery in the face of the foe! One can but approve the austere severity of the great commanders who discouraged the generous impulse of these boys thus lavish of the treasure of their lives. War provides the leaders of men with enough occasions for useful sacrifice without taking it upon themselves to invite a fatal ending. But we must not overlook the fact that these leaders of men are but boys. Sudden stress of circumstances has called them to the battlefront. They feel a necessity for establishing their leadership. But how? By their superior knowledge or experience? No means is open to them except through gallantry in attempting some deed of exceptional daring.

That is evidently the idea which one of them, Georges Bosredon, a twenty-year-old Saint-Cyrien, had in mind when in writing to his sister he puts the matter thus forcibly:

"Say nothing about it to Father and Mother, but, as an officer, I run small chance of returning. I fully recognize this and gladly from this hour offer my life as a sacrifice. We shall arrive at the front very young, with nothing especial to recommend us, to be put in command of men who have seen service, already old soldiers. To keep them going we shall have to give all we have and we shall give it."

Generous-hearted youth, who makes no mention of mistakes made before he was born, and who, just arriving upon the scene, accepts as only natural that he should pay with his life for victory!

In all our great schools and in all our colleges the boys are brothers to these young military commanders. To them all one thing alone is of importance: that France should no longer remain a vanquished nation. These are the young, the pure, the source of new life, the sacrificial offering of their native land. They stand ready to accept any burden laid upon them to render them worthy of their forefathers, to fulfill their destiny and to ransom France.

The college professors made no mistake in judging of them. For some years they had heralded the oncoming of a generation of clear-eyed youths, with confident bearing and hearts knowing no fear. Destiny was preparing deliverers for France. "Whence issues the France of August 2nd?" exclaims one of the masters of the Lycée Janson-de-Sailly.* "From beneath the threat of Germany under which it has been bowed down for forty years. This anguish, this prolonged humiliation, gives place at last to highest hopes."

Such are the young men of our nation. But war has brought together into the army the entire male population from eighteen to forty-eight years of age.

Naturally a man of forty does not leave home with that intoxication of happiness that we have just observed in our young Saint-Cyriens. He no longer feels that "criminal love of danger" which Tolstoi, talking near the end of his long life with Déroulède, acknowledged to have himself felt in his youth. This is due in part to the cooling of the blood; it is also due to the opening up of a new horizon.

*M. S. Rocheblave.

In starting a home of his own the young man of yesterday has taken upon himself certain duties of protection toward his family. How can he be expected to show the magnificent impetuosity of the Saint-Cyrien who says: "To be a young officer during the war is truly the career in which are to be reaped one after another the rewards of honor, energy and devotion."* The father of a family has already gathered to himself the rewards of life; he has to forsake them and, if he fails in the beauty of alacrity, what he manifests is the beauty of a sacrifice always contemplated. This sense of the sacrifice he is making is felt also by the younger man, but he hastily dismisses apprehension on this score, will not admit it so much as to himself, and meeting it face to face, rejects it with anger. The older soldier, on the contrary, welcomes it and regards it as meritorious, it may be as an offering to God, or it may be as an offering to his native land.

*Jean Allard-Méeus in a letter to his mother.

Gemens spero was the motto assumed in the mud of the Artois trenches, by the soldier François Laurentie, the father of six children. He indeed suffered, but was cheered by the hope that his offspring would not have to suffer. All testamentary letters issuing from the trenches echo the same refrain. The Territorial fights that his children may not be called upon to fight. He makes war to abolish war.

But he fights also for his native land. What must have been the feeling of the men of the Twentieth Corps shedding their blood before Nancy and before Verdun! And we can picture the emotion of the men of Péguy, those citizens of the Belleville and Bercy quarters of Paris, when, at the end of their retreat in September, 1914, they caught sight of the great city enveloped in mist,—Paris, to whose defence they were hastening. One of these, Victor Boudon, who had been wounded at the Battle of the Ourcq, writes on that occasion: "From afar we could discern the white rays of the searchlights on the forts of Paris and, from time to time, through the foliage the lights of the capital itself. Our hearts beat violently with joy and with dread."

Another soldier, a shrewd observer of these beginnings of the campaign, thus sums up his testimony: "An all-pervading atmosphere of devout offering."

And what does the war make of these youths and old men? A brotherhood. Binet-Valmer, enlisted as a volunteer for the duration of the war, sends me from the front where he is fighting this most wonderful phrase, which echoes the feeling of all: "Our men are worthy of unstinted admiration, *and we all love one another.*"

The men are admirable, that is to say, they are ready to sacrifice themselves. Behold these soldiers volunteering for the most perilous services,— soldiers who go of their own motion to carry off wounded comrades from between the trenches and to bury the dead;

it is needless to enumerate such occurrences or to present proof of them. It is recognized that the sons of France are brave. And throughout the world everyone knows about the battle which has been going on for five months and which we may rightfully call the victory of Verdun.

But, it may be urged, the men in the other armies also are brave.

A striking fact, and one which especially impressed your great Rudyard Kipling as glorious to a degree seen nowhere else, is the attachment felt by the French soldiers to their commanders, and by the officers to their men, and the loyalty of all to one another.

Between them no falsehood is possible. In that life truth prevails among all. At the outset there was some evidence of extreme republicanism (*sansculottisme*), a sort of scoffing spirit in which there survived in the citizen soldier an excessive feeling of independence in his attitude toward his commander. But since that time, under experiences and trials shared together, this dangerous feeling has been developed and ennobled; while these men preserve toward one another an attitude of criticism as severe as ever, they have adopted as a standard of measurement the service rendered to the common good. They no longer cleave to any but those manifesting actual superiority, whether of mind or heart.

In the midst of the carnage these sons of France constantly recall to mind that they are men with souls. The best of them raise their bloody hands toward Heaven each invoking his God. Each one of them is taken up with trying to show the nobility of his thought through his gallantry and self-sacrifice. Each acts as if he knew (and he does know) that the people of his faith throughout all France have entrusted to his safekeeping their honor and the fortunes of the ideal for which they all are striving. Our schoolmasters vie with our priests in their efforts, while the *élite* of the nation and their brothers in arms join in admiration equally apportioned between them.

Père Gironde writes in his private diary: "To so conduct myself that we cannot again be sent into exile." And Hervé's paper publishes, every day, letters forming a cult in themselves, in which the Socialists voice the question: "What reproach can henceforth be brought against us? Is our faith in internationalism sufficiently justified now it has given us the firm will to save France?"

All are actuated by a lofty moral purpose: the pride and necessity of shedding their blood only in a just cause.

To lift us to the heights where dwell the soldiers of this war what nobler example of spiritual helpfulness toward one another could be afforded than the devotion shown by Lieutenant Colonel Driant? At the peril of his life Driant made his way to the side of one of his lieutenants lying wounded, and under fire of the enemy received his confession and gave him absolution.

The soil of the trenches is holy ground; it is saturated with blood, it is saturated with spirituality.

This intimate brotherhood, this community of spirit, continuing throughout two years of warfare, results in giving to certain military units a collective soul. Certain among these souls are characterized by such nobility, sending forth a radiance comparable to that of the Saints, that other groups receive an increment to their own spirit as a result, simply, of admiration of the qualities thus demonstrated.

"It was in Artois, in the spring of 1915," as a young soldier, Roland Engerand, related to me; "my regiment was coming from a quiet sector on the Aisne where we had sustained few losses. The day before we had received further re-enforcement from the class of 1915. We had been completely fitted out with new clothing. Our horizon-blue uniforms had not had time to be defaced by mud, dust and rain; we were overflowing with enthusiasm; proudly, with full complement of officers and an officer or provisional officer at the head of each section, our columns, three thousand two hundred strong, stretched out along the way. We had been told that we were going to a sacred spot whither all eyes were turned. The opening, so long dreamed of, had been virtually made some hours before, owing to unheard-of feats of heroism performed by the 'Iron' and 'Bronze' divisions. We were to relieve these troops and, as we climbed to the trenches by the loveliest of twilights, we began to ask ourselves with some disquiet whether we could rise to such heights of valor, for it is no light matter to come next in succession to such a record. And, suddenly, upon the road before us, illumined by the setting sun which turned every object to gold, there appeared a sturdy group. Soldiers were approaching, slowly, without haste and without noise; men in rags, still clad in the old dark-blue uniforms, much torn and soiled with mire and blood; guns fouled and rusty; shoes unworthy the name; red *képis,* ill-concealed by tatters of blue coverings, and, amidst all of this, superb countenances, dirty, unshaven, with the poor features drawn and stiffened and eyes whose gaze penetrated to our very souls, for therein were reflected all the sublime sights witnessed during the two weeks just passed. What radiance emanated from these faces of ecstatic suffering and victory! They passed close to us, these men; looking upon us with curiosity, marveling at our luxurious appointments and at our numbers, and, while filing past, said to us simply: 'Don't worry. Keep up your courage; they're done for.' All joined in saying: 'They're done for.' There were voices amongst these distinguishable as young, voices of Parisians, voices of harsher accent, voices from the east, and, at the last, the voice with an Alsatian accent which flung out to us from the rear rank: *'Les Bauches,* they're done for.' That was all that they recalled after all their sufferings. Their captain looked upon them in silence with an expression of wondrous affection.

"And while we, much moved by this encounter, advanced up the slope to take their place, they disappeared from sight with their weary, triumphant step.

"That day I understood what the real beauty of glory is."

What sublimity in the last word uttered by this boy! It is thus that hearts of true nobility are set aflame by contact with heroism. It is thus that the spirit of the population along the eastern border of France, instilled into the Twentieth Corps at its inception and perpetuated by it, circulates among other souls, kindling them into flame.

And sometimes this aggregate soul finds voice.

To-day throughout the world everyone knows about an incident which innumerable newspaper and magazine articles, prints and poems have brought before the public. Doubtless you will recall it. The Germans had entered a trench and shattered all resistance; our soldiers lay stretched to earth, when, suddenly, from this heap of dead and wounded, one arises and, seizing a sack of grenades within reach of his hand, cries out: "To your feet, ye dead men." With a rush the invader is swept back. The inspired word had caused a resurrection.

I was anxious to know the hero of this immortal deed,—Lieutenant Péricard. Here is the tale as he told it to me:

"It was at the Bois-Brulé early in April, 1915. We had been fighting for three days; there was only a handful of worn-out men left of us in the trench, absolutely cut off, with a rain of grenades descending upon our heads. If the Boches had known how few we were! Their artillery raged incessantly. A lieutenant, whose name I cannot now recall, and who had come to my support, stood puffing at his cigarette and laughing at the projectiles, when a bullet struck him just above the temple. He leaned against the parapet, his arms crossed behind him, his head bent slightly forward. From the wound the blood gushes out describing a parabola, like wine through a gimlet-hole in the cask. The head drops further and further forward, then the body, then, all at once, he drops.

"You should have seen the anguish of his men, who threw themselves sobbing upon his body! . . . It was impossible to take a step without treading upon a corpse. Suddenly the precariousness of my situation comes over me. The frenzy which had transported me drops away. I am afraid. I throw myself behind a heap of sacks. The soldier Bonnot remains alone. He gives no heed to anything, but continues to fight like a lion, single-handed against what numbers!

"I pull myself together; his example has shamed me. A few comrades rejoin us. The day draws to a close. We cannot remain as we are. To the right there is still no one in sight. I can look along the trench for a distance of thirty meters, where it is broken into by an enormous bomb-proof. Supposing I should go and see what is going on over beyond there! I hesitate. Then, with one resolute effort, the decision is made.

"The trench is filled with bodies of French soldiers. Blood everywhere. At the first I step forward warily, very uneasy. What! I alone among all these dead men? Then, little by little, I grow bolder. I venture to look at these bodies and I seem to see their eyes fixed upon me. From our own trench, behind me, men are gazing at me with horror in their eyes in which I can read: 'He will surely get killed.' It is true that from the screen of their shelter trenches the Boches are redoubling their efforts. Their grenades are falling all about and the avalanche is fast approaching. I turn back toward the bodies stretched out on the earth. I can but think: 'Then their sacrifice is all to be in vain. It will have been to no avail that these men have fallen. And the Boches will come back. And they will steal our dead from us!' . . . I was transported with rage. Of what I did or precisely what I said I no longer have any clear recollection. I only know that I called out something about like this: 'Come on there! Get up! What are you doing lying there? Let's chase these swine out of here.'

"'To your feet, ye dead men!' Was it raving madness? No. *For the dead replied*. They said to me: 'We follow you.' And, rising at my call, their souls mingled with mine and formed a flaming mass, a mighty stream of molten metal. Nothing could now astonish or hinder me. I had the faith which removes mountains. My voice, hoarse and frayed with calling out orders during the two days and night, had come back to me, clear and strong.

"What took place then? Since I want to tell you only of what I can myself recall, leaving out of account what has been related to me afterward, I must frankly own that I do not know. There is a gap in my recollections; action has consumed memory. I have but a vague idea of a disordered offensive attack in which Bonnot, always in the front rank, stands out clearly from the others. One of the men of my section, though wounded in the arm, never ceased hurling upon the enemy grenades stained with his blood. As for myself, it seems as if I had been given a body which had grown and expanded inordinately,—the body of a giant, with superabundant, limitless energy, extraordinary facility of thought which enabled me to have my eye in ten places at a time,—to call out an order to one man while indicating an order to another by gesture,—to fire a gun and protect myself at the same time from a threatening grenade.

"A prodigious intensity of life coupled with extraordinary episodes! On two occasions we ran completely out of grenades, and on two occasions we discovered full sacks of them at our feet, mixed in with the sandbags. All day long we had been walking over them without seeing them. But no doubt it was the dead who had placed them there! . . .

"At last the Boches began to calm down; we had a chance to consolidate our barricade of sacks farther along in the trench. We were again masters of the situation in our angle.

"Throughout the evening and for several days following I remained under the influence of the spiritual emotion by which I had been carried away at the time of the summons to the dead. I had something of the same feeling that one has after partaking fervently of the communion. I recognized that I had just been living through such hours as I should never see again, during which my head, having by violent exertion broken an opening through the ceiling, had risen into the region of the supernatural, into the invisible world peopled by gods and heroes.

"At that moment, certainly, I was lifted up above myself. It must have been so, for I received the congratulations of my men upon it. To any one who has lived in company with the *poilus* there is no Legion of Honor which is to be compared in value to such congratulations.

"If, in telling you of these events, I seem to you to be seeking satisfaction to my vanity, it is because I have ill-expressed my feeling and my intention. I well know that there is nothing of the hero about me. Every time that I have had to leap over the parapet I have shivered with fright, and the terror with which I was seized in the press of battle, of which I told you a few moments ago, is not an accidental occurrence in my life as a soldier. I have earned no approbation of any sort. It was the living who carried me along by their example, and the dead who led me by the hand. The summons did not issue from the lips of a man, but from the hearts of all those lying prostrate there, living and dead. One man alone could not strike the keynote. For that is needed the collaboration of many souls uplifted by circumstances, of whom some had already begun their flight into eternity.

"Why was it that I was chosen rather than some officer or some soldier among those who were concerned in the affair, —one whose courage had not, like mine, known faltering? Why was it I rather than Colonel de Belnay, who ran up and down the lines under a downpour of grenades; or Lieutenant Erlaud, or Sub-lieutenant Pellerin, or Provisional Officer Vignaud, or Sergeant Prot, or Corporal Chuy, or Corporal Thévin, or Private Bonnot? (He went on to mention an endless number besides these.) Wherefore? Because one may receive inspiration from above and yet be only a poor ordinary man.

"If ever you tell this tale I adjure you to give the names of all these commanders and these soldiers, for it would be an untruth to make it seem as if I were monopolizing the glory of our regiment's great day. The summons was not mine alone, it was that of us all. The more you sink my part in the whole mass, the nearer you will come to actual fact. I am firmly persuaded of having been only an instrument in the hands of a power above."

II

Here are the facts. Here at least is a sample,—a sample of the wine which for two years has been fermenting on our hills, of the wheat of our furrows and of the blood of our battles.

But in all this is there, after all, anything unheard-of or unexpected? It is fruit produced by France, similar to that which this ancient nation has yielded so many times throughout the centuries of her existence; it is the wine, the wheat, the blood of all our epics. We may recognize in our past a prototype of each one of the qualities and exploits which we have just observed. The heroic poems (*Chansons de Geste*), the Crusades, all the early years of France, abound with innumerable deeds achieved by our knights and by the *Sancta Plebs Dei* which, in anticipation, usher in the feats inscribed in our army reports in 1916.

The mortal vow of the young Saint-Cyriens—why that is a typical episode of our *Chansons de Geste*. There is no theme which they develop with greater freshness and spirit than the warlike alacrity, purity and willing obedience of the young heroes, the Aymerillots, the Rolands, Guy de Bourgognes in their early adolescence.

When the *Montmirails* and the *Croix du Drapeaus* take their oath to undergo their baptism of fire wearing white gloves and with the plume in their *képis,* it is a chapter of the *"Enfances Vivien"* brought to life again.

On the day when the young Vivien assumes the arms of a knight he swears before his assembled family never to give ground the length of his spear in battle, and it is owing to that oath that he comes to his death.

Gemens spero; this is the thought which the recollection of his six children inspires in the Territorial; he takes mournful satisfaction in calling them to mind. A parallel case to the knight of whom Jacques de Vitry tells us, who, at the moment of his departure for the Crusade, assembles his children about him. "I had them all come," he explains, "so that my grief at parting should be the more poignant and thus make offering to God of a greater sacrifice."

The sense of equality and brotherhood prevailing in our trenches. . . . Joinville relates that Saint Louis worked in the trenches and himself shouldered the carrying-basket.

"None is base until his actions prove him base."

(*Nuls n'est vilains s'il ne fait vilenie.*)

This is a line from the *Chansons de Geste,* as it might equally well have been a line from Corneille, as it likewise is the thought of every man and woman in France in 1916. During the Battle of Antioch the Bishop of Puy thus addressed the Crusaders:

"We who are all baptized in the name of Christ are all the sons of God and brothers one of another. . . . Let us wage war, then, in the same spirit, as brothers." And, again, it is the Sire de Bourlémont who speaks. (Now Bourlémont is the Seigniory over Domrémy, Jeanne d'Arc's birthplace, and the Sire de Bourlémont, he whose grandson was destined later to know Jeanne d'Arc.) To Joinville, who was starting for the Crusade, the Sire de Bourlémont gave utterance to these words:

"Ye are about to betake yourselves to lands beyond the seas; now it behooves you to take thought against the time of your return, for no Chevalier, be he poor or rich, may return without suffering disgrace if he leave in the hands of the Saracens *the lowly people of our Lord* in whose company he journeyed forth."

Driant crawling through the storm of shot and shell to carry absolution to a dying lieutenant. It is the same story as that of William of Orange coming to the rescue of his nephew Vivien at the Battle of Aliscamps. He is too late in getting there, he fights at great length to reach him, does not succeed in finding him either alive or dead. Evening comes on. He rides about the field, very weary. From his brow, encircled by the band of his helmet, drops of blood fall as from the crown of thorns. He searches in vain for Vivien. At last upon the grass at his feet he recognizes the boy's shield, bristling with arrows. Further on, not far from a spring, under the spreading branches of a huge olive tree, lies Vivien insensible, his pallid hands crossed upon his breast. William dismounts, clasps him all bleeding in his arms and weeps over him as one dead. "Nephew Vivien, lovely youth, this is a piteous end to your deeds of prowess just begun." But, little by little, the boy in his arms shows signs of life, he opens his eyes; he had "kept his hold on life," knowing that William would come. Having given praise to God, William of Orange asks whether Vivien desires to make avowal of his sins to him as a "true confession." "I am thy uncle, no one here is nearer to thee than I, save God alone; in his stead and place I will be thy chaplain; I will stand sponsor to thee at this baptism." Vivien makes confession; the one great sin upon his soul is that of having fled, as he believes, contrary to his vow. William absolves him, then, taking the consecrated wafer from his alms-bag, administers the sacrament to the dying youth. Vivien gives up the ghost. Night has come, William could now make his escape alone across the hostile lines. And yet, when the moment comes for leaving the body there, he is seized with compunction. Desert him thus alone in the gloom! When other fathers lose their sons in death do they not keep watch above their bodies through the night? He proceeds to tie his horse to the olive tree and begins his vigil. Under the dense shade Vivien's body diffuses a radiance and a perfume as of balm and myrrh. The night is mild and tranquil. Standing beside the body of his dead boy the count weeps, he cannot sate his mind with what he beholds, and, letting pass the dawn, he waits until the sun be completely above the horizon and shining brightly. Then, having repaired the broken latchets of his helmet, he once more kissed his nephew's face and gazed upon it for the last time. Mounting into the saddle he took his way slowly toward the road held by the Saracens until within bow-shot of the enemy when, shouting his battle-cry, he charged with his ashen lance in rest.

To your feet, ye dead men! Surely we have heard before the wonder-working summons of the Bois d'Ailly. At the siege of Ascalon the Templars behold, exposed above the gate of the city, a number of their brethren, hanged by the Saracens. They are filled with despondency and are for raising the siege; which seeing, the Grand Master of the Templars said to them: "Behold the dead are calling to us, for already they have taken the city."

It would be possible to multiply to infinity the number of these similarities, these meeting points between the younger France and the France of to-day, held by some to be past its prime. Designers of the stained glass in our cathedrals have frequently placed figures from the ancient Scriptures in juxtaposition to those of the new; here Jonah and the whale, there Christ and the tomb; here Moses and the burning bush, there the Virgin beside the manger; so I, in like manner, might call to mind instances without number, following the same rule of symmetry for setting off the likeness between the grandsons and their forefathers, and, to go still deeper, the correspondences between this war and all our other wars.

THE UNDYING SPIRIT OF FRANCE 43

We already knew the Zouave of 1914 who, from the middle of a group of prisoners behind which the Germans were sheltering themselves, called out to the French soldiers: "Fire ahead!" and died, riddled by their bullets. It was nine centuries before his time that the Saracens compelled a prisoner taken from the Crusaders to mount the battlements of Antioch that he might from there entreat his brethren to give up the assault upon the city. Instead he called to them to make the attack and the Saracens revenged themselves by cutting off his head. Etienne de Bourbon adds to the tale that the head, thrown from the top of the walls by a ballista, came into the hands of the Christians where it was noted that the countenance wore a smile of joy.

Between these two comes the Chevalier d'Assas, the young soldier so terribly disfigured, who said: "If my father should see me now! But what does it matter! He did not beget me to be handsome, he begot me to be brave," into which assertion he evidently put the same pride as Montluc in enumerating his seven arquebuse wounds, of which the most admirable to his mind was that of Rabastens which had torn a hole in his face.

And, again, there was Captain de F—— who averred that: "An officer of my rank who does his duty under the circumstances in which I am placed should not return alive," evidence of a spirit of sacrifice surpassing the word of command given by Godfrey de Bouillon at the time of the last assault against Jerusalem at David's Gate: "Seek not to avoid death, go rather in search of it."

The poet Charles Perrot was killed before Arras on the twenty-third of October; one of his comrades, perceiving that he was ill, said to him: "I am going to take your place. You have done your full duty. Go and get some rest." To which Perrot replied: "There is no end to doing one's duty." This modern poet was of the same mind

THE UNDYING SPIRIT OF FRANCE 45

as the Chevalier Erard de Sivry who fought at the side of Joinville in a ruined house at Mansurah with five other chevaliers completing the garrison. Horribly wounded in the face he hesitates at going to seek assistance lest some day discredit should result to him and his kindred. "You may well go," Joinville assured him, "for already you are a dead man"; but he was not to be satisfied with Joinville's opinion, he felt that he must ask counsel one by one of each of the others.

In the wood of La Grurie a company of the 151st Regiment of Infantry bars the entrance to the trench. Three men only can stand abreast at that spot. As fast as one falls another takes his place. The combat lasts for two hours; thirty men thus give up their lives. The incident is a commonplace, one of almost daily occurrence.

One cannot fail to be reminded of that episode of the Crusades known as *"le Pas Saladin,"* which was everywhere commemorated and depicted in castle halls. It was your King Richard, Gautier de Châtillon, Guillaume des Barres and nine other knights who were holding this defile before Jaffa. Throughout the Middle Ages these twelve men were looked upon as very mirrors of chivalry, and their armorial bearings were preserved as precious relics. But we shall never know the names of the grenadiers of the wood of La Grurie and of so many other trenches. There are too many of them.

III

For more than a thousand years now this mighty stream of feats of valor has been flowing in undiminished volume. We have just been dipping into it; we could carry away from the passing flood only what could be contained in our two hands held together. And what about it all? What is proved by these entrancing and heroic achievements, this life beneath the surface, this overflowing French spirit?

The French make war as a religious duty. They were the first to formulate the idea of a holy war. The soldier of the year II, believing himself the bearer of liberty and equality to a captive world, dedicated himself with the same zeal and in the same spirit as the Crusaders to Jerusalem. When the Crusader shouts "God wills it," when the volunteer at Valmy shouts "The Republic calls us," it is but another form of the same battle-cry. The idea is that of bringing about more of justice and more of beauty in the world. To both a voice from Heaven or their conscience speaks, saying:

"If you die, you will be holy martyrs."*

It is not in France that wars are entered upon for the sake of the spoils. Wars for the sake of honor and glory? Yes, at times. But to carry the nation with it the people must feel itself a champion in the cause of God, a knight

*Se vous mourez, esterez sainz martirs. La Chanson de Roland.—Archbishop Turpin before the battle, to the army on its knees.

upholding justice. We have to be convinced that we are contending against Barbarians,—in former days against Islam, at the present time against Pan Germanism, or against the despotic Prussian militarism and German imperialism.

Frenchmen fighting in defence of their country have believed almost always that they were suffering and enduring that all humanity might be the better. They fight for their territory filled with sepulchers and for Heaven where Christ reigns, and up to which at least our aspirations rise. They die for France, as far as the purposes of France may be identified with the purposes of God or indeed with those of humanity. Thus it is that they wage war in the spirit of martyrs.

Would you have me present to your minds a wonderful theme; would you know how our forefathers, nine centuries ago, were persuaded to go on Crusade? You would learn at the same time how our soldiers of the present day ought to be addressed. Listen to the words of Pope Urban II (a native of France, born in Champagne) as he preached before the Council of Clermont in Auvergne: "People of France," he said, "nation elect of God, as is shown by your deeds, and beloved of God, distinguished above all others by your devotion to the holy faith and to the Church, it is to you that our word and our exhortation is directed. . . . Upon whom may be laid the task of avenging the outrageous acts of the Unbelievers if not upon you, Frenchmen, to whom God has vouchsafed more than to any other people, illustrious distinction in arms, exalted hearts and agile bodies with the power to bend those who oppose you? May your souls be stirred and quickened by the deeds of your ancestors, the valor and might of your King Charlemagne, of his son Louis, and of your other kings, who have overthrown the dominion of the heathen and extended the confines of the Holy Church! . . . O very valiant knights, offspring of an invincible lineage, recall to mind the prowess of your fathers!" That was the right way to put things before our noble ancestors. And that is how they were pleaded with by Jeanne d'Arc, who called herself "the Daughter of God" (*Fille Dieu*). Bonaparte adopted the same tone and with him the republican generals, and it is still the same spirit with which the hearts of our soldiers are kindled when they rush forward out of the trenches singing the *Marseillaise* under the benison of their chaplains.

Doubtless reason does its part in affecting and convincing us. The argument is used that France is a real and tangible masterpiece whose outline must be perfected and maintained, that Strasbourg and Metz are essential to her existence, that she needs to establish the balance to her southern population by accessions to the north and east, that she will be as if disarmed and open to attack as long as she remains deprived of her natural frontiers. But this would still leave many apathetic. To be ready to sacrifice their lives the sons of France demand that they shall not die for the cause of France alone.

There came a time when France burst the chain of her traditions and lost from sight even her memories of the past; nevertheless to her spiritual nature she still remained faithful. In each succeeding generation she has brought forth Rolands, Godfreys of Bouillon, Bayards, Turennes, Marceaus, unfamiliar as these names might have become, and at all times she is elate with sentiments which vary only in form of expression.

The epic drowses at times, but never, from the beginning, was it more fired by brotherly love and zeal for religion than at the present hour. Many passages from the Old Testament, obscure and of small moment in themselves, do not reveal their full meaning except in the light of the New, so the feats of valor performed by knights of old and our revered ancestors seem but the prefiguration of richer and holier things of to-day. The entire history of our nation would appear to have been leading up to what we have witnessed during the past two years.

Millions of Frenchmen have entered this war with a fervor of heroism and martyrdom which formerly, in the most exalted epochs of our history, characterized only the flower of the combatants. Young or old, poor or rich, and whatever his religious faith, the French soldier of 1916 knows that his is a nation which intervenes when injustice prevails upon the earth, and in his muddy trench, gun in hand, he knows that he is carrying onward the *Gesta Dei per Francos*.

Roland, on the evening after Roncevaux, murmurs with dying breath: "O Land of France, most sweet art thou, my country." It is with similar expressions and the same love that our soldiers of to-day are dying. *"Au revoir,"* writes Jean Cherlomey to his wife, "promise me to bear no grudge against

France if she requires all of me."—"*Au revoir*, it is for the sake of France," were the dying words of Captain Hersart de La Villemarqué.—"*Vive la France*, I am well content, I am dying for her sake," said Corporal Voituret of the Second Dragoons, and expired while trying to sing the *Marseillaise*.—Albert Malet, whose handbooks are used in teaching history to our school children, enlisted for the war; his chest is pierced by a bullet, he shouts: "Forward, my friends! I am happy in dying for France," and sinks upon the barbed wire in front of the enemy's trenches.—"*Vive la France*, I die, but I am well content," cry in turn, one after another, thousands of dying men, and the soldier Raissac of the Thirty-first of the line, mortally wounded on the twenty-third of September, 1914, finds strength before expiring to write on the back of his mother's photograph: "It is an honor for the French soldier to die."

They do not wish to be mourned. Georges Morillot, a graduate of the

Ecole Normale and sub-lieutenant in the Twenty-seventh Infantry, died for France in the forest of Apremont on December 11, 1914, leaving a letter to his parents: "If this letter comes into your hands it will be because I am no more and because I shall have died the most glorious of deaths. Do not bewail me too much; my end is of all the most to be desired. . . . Speak of me from time to time as of one of those who have given their blood that France may live and who have died gladly. . . . Since my earliest childhood I have always dreamed of dying for my country, my face toward the foe. . . . Let me sleep where the accident of battle shall have placed me, by the side of those who, like myself, shall have died for France; I shall sleep well there. . . . My dear Father and Mother, happy are they who die for their native land. What matters the life of individuals if France is saved? My dearly-beloved, do not grieve. . . . *Vive la France!*"—Louis Belanger, twenty years of age, killed by the enemy on September 28, 1915, had written to his family: "I hope that my death will not be to you a cause of sorrow, but an occasion for pride. It is my wish that mourning should not be worn for me, for, in the glorious day when France shall be restored the sombre garb must not be allowed to dull the sunlight with which all French souls will be irradiated." In obedience to his desire the cards announcing his death were not framed in black, but edged with silver. Hubert Prouvé-Drouot was a Saint-Cyrien of the class called *La Grande Revanche*, who died on the field of honor; when leaving home to join his regiment he makes this his last request to his mother: "When the troops come home victorious through the *Arc de Triomphe*, if I am no longer amongst them, put on your finest apparel and be there."

The mothers understand and share this sacred enthusiasm. Beside the hospital bed, where lies extended the body of his dead son, a father weeps; the mother, a peasant woman, takes him by the hand: "We have got to have courage, my husband. You see well enough the boy had it."—A soldier from Bagnères-de-Bigorre, a gardener at Lourdes, sorely wounded, died at the hospital maintained by l'Institut de France; his wife, summoned by telegram, arrives too late. Before the body lying cold in death she said simply: "He died for his country, she was his mother, I am only his wife."—Madame de Castelnau, the wife of the illustrious general, while at the communion table was praying for her three sons at the front when she observed that the hand of the priest presenting her with the wafer was trembling. She understood and said simply: "Which one?"

The fact is that the French mothers, sustained by a power above, believe that their sons, in yielding their lives for France, find, not death, but an evolution. One of them, who is unwilling that her name should be given, uses this word in a letter radiant with sacred beauty.

Paris, October 20, 1915.
"Commandant,

"I cannot thank you adequately for the accuracy of your sorrowful recollections. The anniversary of the sacrifice of my brave boy is at the same time particularly cruel and particularly sweet; cruel, because it recalls to mind a day when I was thinking of him, without misgivings as to the anguish which his valor was to cost me; sweet, because I could not visualize the abrupt end of this pure and brief life under any other aspect than that of a supreme evolution.

"I thank you, Commandant, for all that you tell me of my dear young soldier; may his glorious death contribute to the victory of our country; when that time comes I shall kneel and once more say 'I thank you.' My mother's heart remains shattered in face of the death of this boy of twenty years who was all my joy. Oh, how proud and how unhappy one can be at the same time!

"Will you, Commandant, allow me to

transmit through you my tender feeling toward all those who cherish a remembrance of him who has fallen in his country's defence, and say to them that my thoughts turn frequently to that Land of Lorraine, so dear to all French hearts?"

"A supreme evolution," she says. It would seem, indeed, that we have known only the chrysalis form and that an entire people is unfolding its wings. The ever-living France is freeing herself. It is for her that the sons of France are dying a death devoutly accepted by their mothers.

A woman of the common people receives notification of the death of her husband on the field of honor while she is holding in her arms her babe to whom she is giving nourishment. She reels, straightens up again and cries: *"Vive la France,"* holding up her son toward Heaven. Child of martyrs, offspring of thirty generations of such, thou shalt live to-morrow in a victorious France.